Joe Cavill

Somatic Trauma Therapy

10-Minute Proven Exercises for Trauma Recovery and Anxiety Relief

First edition

This book was professionally typeset on Reedsy
Find out more at reedsy.com

Contents

1.

2.

3.

4.

5.

6.

7.

8.

9.

10.

11.

12.

13.

14.

15.

16.

17.

18.

19.

20.

21.

22.

23.

24.

25.

26.

I

Part 1: Understanding Somatic Trauma Therapy

1

Introduction to Somatic Trauma Therapy

You see, Sarah had always considered herself resilient—until one day, the weight of her unresolved trauma began to show. An unexpected panic attack in the grocery store left her trembling. The sights, sounds, and smells triggered memories she thought she had buried. Years of pushing down her past, trying to survive in silence, had finally caught up with her.

Traditional talk therapy helped her understand her emotions, but something was still missing. She needed more than words to feel safe again. That's when Sarah discovered somatic therapy.

It started with simple exercises like grounding, where she would plant her feet on the floor and focus on her breath. Over time, she learned how to notice her body's signals—the tightness in her chest when fear crept in, the tension in her shoulders when anger simmered, or the heaviness in her stomach when sadness overwhelmed her. Through somatic techniques, Sarah began to release the trauma stored in her body, bit by bit. These practices became her lifeline, helping her reclaim control over her emotions and reconnect with herself.

Somatic therapy was the missing piece that allowed Sarah not only to understand her trauma but to feel it, release it, and heal.

This book is dedicated to that same journey—one of releasing stored pain and reclaiming emotional resilience. You will discover the power of somatic therapy in combination with other therapeutic approaches like mindfulness and cognitive-behavioral therapy (CBT), empowering you to truly heal from within.

Trauma has a profound impact not only on the mind but also on the body. While traditional therapies focus on mental and emotional healing, somatic trauma therapy offers a unique, body-centered approach to trauma recovery. This chapter introduces somatic trauma therapy, explains its principles, and explores its numerous benefits. We'll also clarify how somatic awareness plays a crucial role and examine why this form of therapy is distinct from other modalities.

What is Somatic Trauma Therapy?

Somatic trauma therapy is a form of therapy that recognizes trauma as a full-body experience, not just a psychological one. It works on the principle that trauma gets stored in the body as physical tension or discomfort, leading to chronic stress, anxiety, and other emotional or physical symptoms. This type of therapy focuses on releasing the trauma by involving the body in the healing process.

Instead of only talking about trauma, somatic therapy encourages you to tune into the physical sensations in your body—whether it's a tightness in your chest, a knot in your stomach, or tension in your shoulders. Through a combination of breathing exercises, mindful movement, and gentle body awareness techniques, individuals can process and release the trauma that has been stored in their body for years.

This can seem abstract at first, especially if you're used to thinking of therapy as something that happens through talking and thinking. But as you practice paying attention to the subtle signals your body sends, you begin to unlock patterns of tension and stress, leading to greater emotional and physical relief.

Somatic Awareness: The Key to Healing

At the heart of somatic trauma therapy is the concept of **somatic awareness**—the ability to observe and connect with bodily sensations. When we've experienced trauma, our bodies often hold onto that stress long after the event has passed. Somatic awareness teaches you to gently notice these sensations without judgment, allowing you to reconnect with parts of your body that might have felt "numb" or "frozen" due to trauma.

Imagine you're going through a difficult memory, and your chest feels tight or your stomach feels unsettled. Instead of pushing these sensations away, somatic therapy invites you to notice them and explore what your body is telling you. These physical reactions are often your body's way of signaling unresolved trauma, and by bringing your awareness to them, you can begin to release the hold they have on you.

For example, many people who have experienced trauma find that they hold tension in specific parts of their body—perhaps clenching their jaw or keeping their shoulders raised in a defensive posture. By becoming aware of these physical patterns, somatic trauma therapy helps you unwind that tension and feel more at ease in your own skin.

The Core Principles of Somatic Trauma Therapy

Somatic trauma therapy is guided by several core principles that set it apart from traditional talk therapy:

1. The Body Stores Trauma
2. Trauma leaves an imprint on the body, leading to physical symptoms like muscle tension, chronic pain, or fatigue. Somatic therapy helps release this stored trauma through body-centered techniques.
3. The Mind and Body Are Connected
4. Somatic therapy emphasizes the **interconnectedness** of the mind and body. Healing requires addressing both the emotional and physical aspects of trauma.
5. Somatic Awareness Promotes Healing
6. Developing **somatic awareness** allows individuals to become more in tune with their bodies, helping them identify where trauma is stored and how to release it.
7. The Nervous System and Trauma
8. Trauma often dysregulates the nervous system, leaving individuals in a state of chronic stress or emotional numbness. Somatic techniques help restore balance and calm to the nervous system, facilitating healing.
9. Movement and Mindfulness Are Essential
10. Gentle movements, mindful breathing, and grounding exercises are key components of somatic trauma therapy, helping individuals process trauma in a holistic way.

Common Benefits of Somatic Trauma Therapy

Many people turn to somatic trauma therapy when other approaches haven't fully addressed their trauma symptoms. Here are some common benefits that clients experience through this therapy:

1. Physical and Emotional Release
2. By focusing on bodily sensations, somatic trauma therapy helps release the physical tension and discomfort associated with trauma, leading to relief from

chronic pain, headaches, and muscle tightness. On an emotional level, this release can also lead to greater freedom from anxiety and overwhelm.

3. Improved Emotional Regulation
4. Somatic therapy teaches individuals how to regulate their emotions by tuning into their bodies. As you become more aware of how emotions manifest physically, you gain greater control over emotional responses, which helps reduce anxiety and feelings of being overwhelmed.
5. **Increased Mind-Body Connection**
6. Trauma often disconnects individuals from their bodies, making them feel detached or dissociated. Somatic therapy fosters a greater connection between the mind and body, promoting a sense of wholeness and integration.
7. **Stress and Anxiety Reduction**
8. Somatic techniques, particularly those that focus on calming the nervous system, are effective in reducing symptoms of stress and anxiety. As individuals practice mindful breathing, body awareness, and grounding exercises, they experience greater emotional calm.
9. **Enhanced Relationships**
10. As individuals heal from trauma and improve emotional regulation, they often find that their relationships improve as well. Feeling more connected to themselves enables them to communicate more clearly and develop healthier, more supportive connections with others.

How Somatic Trauma Therapy Differs from Traditional Therapy

Somatic trauma therapy takes a unique approach by integrating the body into the healing process, whereas traditional talk therapy primarily focuses on the mind and emotions. In methods like **cognitive behavioral therapy (CBT)** or **psychodynamic therapy**, the focus is on exploring thoughts, feelings, and behaviors. These approaches can be helpful, but they don't always address how trauma is held in the body.

For instance, while talk therapy might explore why you feel anxious, somatic trauma therapy would ask you to notice where you feel that anxiety in your body. Is there tightness in your chest? A knot in your stomach? By addressing the physical experience of trauma, somatic therapy helps release tension and stored energy that talking alone might not reach.

Additionally, somatic trauma therapy is particularly effective for people who feel "stuck" in their trauma recovery, even after extensive traditional therapy. Because it works with the nervous system, somatic therapy helps individuals access deeper levels of healing by calming and resetting the body's stress response.

A Personal Story: Healing Through Somatic Awareness

Take *Rachel*, for example, who had experienced a traumatic event several years ago. Though she had gone through talk therapy and made significant emotional progress, she still felt chronic tightness in her shoulders and neck. She found herself frequently anxious, especially in crowded places, but couldn't explain why the anxiety persisted.

When Rachel began somatic trauma therapy, her therapist guided her to focus on her body's reactions during stressful situations. Rachel noticed how her muscles tensed when she felt anxious, and how her breath became shallow. By developing this somatic awareness, Rachel was able to consciously release that tension during stressful moments through deep breathing and gentle stretches. Over time, her anxiety reduced, and the tightness in her shoulders became far less severe.

Conclusion

Somatic trauma therapy offers a compassionate, body-centered path to healing trauma. By understanding that trauma is stored not only in the mind but also in the body, this approach allows for deeper, more holistic recovery. Through somatic awareness, mindful movements, and nervous system regulation, individuals can release long-held tension and emotional pain, moving toward a life of greater peace and emotional freedom.

In the following chapters, you'll learn practical techniques and exercises that will help you incorporate somatic therapy into your daily life. Remember, the process of healing takes time—but as you reconnect with your body and gently release stored trauma, you'll discover a profound sense of relief and renewal.

Your body has the wisdom to heal, and somatic trauma therapy is a gentle yet powerful way to tap into that innate resilience.

2

The Science of Somatic Therapy: How trauma affects the body and nervous system

Understanding how trauma affects the body is key to healing through somatic therapy. Trauma impacts not only the mind but also the body's physiological systems, leaving behind imprints that may manifest as chronic stress, physical tension, or emotional numbness. In this chapter, we will explore how trauma alters the body's nervous system, the critical role of the **vagus nerve**, and how these changes influence emotional regulation. By delving into the science behind somatic therapy, you'll gain insight into why it is such an effective approach to trauma recovery.

How Trauma Affects the Body: The Hidden Wounds

Trauma is a deeply embodied experience. When someone goes through a traumatic event, the body reacts instinctively, entering a state of high alert. This is the **fight, flight, or freeze response**, designed to protect us from danger. While this response is natural and necessary in the face of immediate threats, trauma can cause it to become stuck, leading to prolonged states of hypervigilance or shutdown.

Chronic tension, **difficulty sleeping**, and **digestive issues** are just a few ways that trauma can physically manifest. Trauma survivors often report feeling "on edge" or emotionally detached long after the danger has passed. These lingering effects are rooted in how trauma disrupts the body's natural ability to return to a state of calm, leaving both physical and emotional wounds that may be difficult to heal without addressing the body directly.

The Nervous System: Trauma's Battlefield

The **nervous system** is at the heart of how trauma affects the body. To understand somatic therapy's role in healing, it's essential to first grasp the two key branches of the nervous system involved in trauma responses:

- **Sympathetic Nervous System (SNS)**: When the SNS is activated during a traumatic event, it prepares the body for action—whether that's fighting the threat or running away from it. This is the fight-or-flight response. The body floods with adrenaline, heart rate increases, and muscles tense. The SNS plays an important role in survival, but when it becomes overactive due to unresolved trauma, it can lead to chronic stress and anxiety.
- **Parasympathetic Nervous System (PNS)**: This branch of the nervous system is responsible for rest and recovery. After the threat passes, the PNS should calm the body down, slowing the heart rate and reducing stress hormones. However, in people who have experienced trauma, the PNS often struggles to regain control, leaving them stuck in a cycle of heightened stress or emotional shutdown.

Somatic therapy works by directly engaging the **PNS**, helping the body to relearn how to shift from a state of high alert to one of relaxation. Through somatic practices like mindful breathing, body scanning, and movement, trauma survivors can restore the balance between the SNS and PNS, allowing their nervous system to return to its natural rhythm.

The Vagus Nerve: A Key to Unlocking Trauma

Central to the body's ability to recover from trauma is the **vagus nerve**, one of the longest nerves in the body, running from the brainstem through the heart, lungs, and digestive tract. The vagus nerve is a core component of the parasympathetic nervous system and plays a crucial role in regulating stress responses, emotional states, and even social connections.

When the vagus nerve is functioning well, it helps the body relax after stress by lowering heart rate, reducing tension, and promoting digestion. But after trauma, the vagus nerve can become dysregulated, making it harder for individuals to calm down or feel emotionally balanced. This dysfunction is one reason why trauma survivors may feel perpetually unsafe or on edge, even in environments that are objectively safe.

Vagal tone, or the health of the vagus nerve, is an essential factor in emotional regulation and trauma recovery. A person with high vagal tone is better able to shift between stress and relaxation, while someone with low vagal tone may find themselves stuck in one extreme or the other—constantly anxious or emotionally numb.

In somatic therapy, **stimulating the vagus nerve** through practices like **deep breathing, humming**, or **gently massaging the neck** can help improve vagal tone, bringing the body back into balance. This allows the nervous system to better manage stress and promotes emotional healing.

Physiological Responses to Trauma: Fight, Flight, Freeze

The body's **fight, flight, or freeze** responses are natural survival mechanisms. But after trauma, these responses can become habitual, creating chronic patterns of emotional and physical distress.

- **Fight**: In this response, the body prepares to confront the threat head-on. Trauma survivors may find themselves experiencing chronic **anger, irritability**, or **muscle tension**, especially in the upper body and jaw. They may feel the need to fight against perceived threats, even when no danger is present.
- **Flight**: The flight response is about escaping danger, physically or emotionally. Those stuck in this response may experience constant **anxiety, restlessness**, or a desire to flee from situations that feel overwhelming. They may have difficulty staying grounded or may avoid stressful situations or relationships.
- **Freeze**: In the freeze response, the body shuts down. Trauma survivors who experience freezing may feel **numb, disconnected**, or **dissociated** from their emotions. They may describe feeling paralyzed by fear or unable to move forward in life.

Somatic therapy helps to **unlock these stuck responses** by engaging the body in safe, mindful movement and relaxation techniques. Through these practices, trauma survivors can teach their nervous systems how to process and release stored tension, rather than remaining trapped in a state of chronic stress or numbness.

Emotional Regulation and Trauma: How the Body Holds Our Feelings

Emotional regulation is often compromised in individuals who have experienced trauma. Many trauma survivors find it difficult to manage their emotions, swinging between states of anxiety and emotional numbness. This is because trauma impacts the body's ability to regulate stress, leaving the nervous system in a state of overdrive or shut down.

The physical sensations that accompany emotions—like a tight chest when anxious or a lump in the throat when sad—are signals from the body that can help us understand and manage our emotional states. However, trauma often disconnects individuals from these sensations, making it harder to recognize and respond to emotions effectively.

Somatic therapy emphasizes the importance of **reconnecting with the body** as a way to regulate emotions. By noticing and responding to physical sensations, trauma survivors can begin to process their feelings in a healthier, more balanced way. Somatic practices like **body scanning** or **grounding exercises** help individuals tune into their bodies, allowing them to release tension and regain control over their emotional states.

Sarah's Path to Recovery

To see how somatic therapy can make a difference, let's look at *Sarah*, a 45-year-old mother who struggled with unresolved trauma from childhood abuse. For years, Sarah experienced frequent panic attacks, migraines, and a sense of disconnection from her own body. She had tried talk therapy, but something was still missing—she couldn't shake the physical tension that gripped her daily life.

When Sarah started somatic trauma therapy, her therapist introduced her to **diaphragmatic breathing** and **body scanning**. Sarah quickly became aware of the tightness she held in her chest and abdomen—places she had never fully noticed before. As she practiced these techniques regularly, she began to feel a sense of calm she hadn't experienced in years.

Within a few months, Sarah's panic attacks decreased, and she felt more in tune with her body. For the first time in a long time, she felt in control of her emotions and her body, rather than feeling like a prisoner to her trauma.

Healing Through Somatic Trauma Therapy

Somatic trauma therapy provides a powerful, body-based approach to healing the deep wounds of trauma. By addressing the physiological effects of trauma, particularly in the **nervous system** and **vagus nerve**, somatic therapy offers a compassionate path to recovery. Techniques that engage the body's natural ability to regulate stress and release tension can help individuals break free from the cycles of chronic distress that trauma creates.

As you continue on your healing journey, remember that your body holds the key to your recovery. With patience, compassion, and the right tools, somatic therapy can guide you toward greater emotional balance, physical relief, and a lasting sense of safety.

3

Somatic Techniques for Trauma Release

Trauma leaves an indelible mark on the body, a silent scream that echoes through every cell. But what if you could unlock the secrets of your own healing? What if the key to releasing stored trauma lay not in talking about it, but in feeling it – in the tension in your shoulders, the knot in your stomach, or the numbness in your heart? In this chapter, we'll explore the transformative power of somatic techniques, from mindfulness and breathwork to movement and body scanning. Through these practices, you'll learn to listen to your body's whispers, and uncover a path to lasting freedom.

Mindfulness: Becoming Aware of the Present Moment

At the heart of many somatic techniques is **mindfulness**, a practice that invites you to bring your awareness to the present moment without judgment. When you experience trauma, your mind often tries to either escape the discomfort by dissociating or gets stuck reliving the past. Mindfulness helps to bridge this gap, allowing you to reconnect with the here and now.

In somatic trauma therapy, mindfulness is used to focus on the **physical sensations** in your body. By gently noticing how your body feels, whether it's tension in your shoulders or a tightness in your chest, mindfulness teaches you to acknowledge these sensations without trying to change or avoid them. This simple awareness can be profoundly healing.

Example: Julia

Julia, a 35-year-old teacher, had struggled with the lingering effects of a car accident. Even though she had physically healed, she continued to feel tense and anxious. In her somatic therapy sessions, her therapist introduced her to **mindful body awareness**. As Julia practiced bringing her attention to her body, she began to notice the areas where she was holding tension—particularly in her chest and abdomen. Over time, she was able to acknowledge these sensations without judgment and release some of the tension through **mindful breathing** and relaxation.

Mindfulness is not about avoiding or fixing your emotions but rather learning to be present with them, allowing the body to do its natural work of healing.

Breathwork

Breathing is something we do automatically, but in somatic trauma therapy, conscious breathwork is used as a tool for calming the nervous system and releasing stored trauma. When we are stressed or afraid, our breathing becomes shallow and rapid, signaling to the body that it's in danger. By engaging in intentional, **deep breathing exercises**, we can send the opposite signal—telling the body that it's safe to relax.

Diaphragmatic breathing, also known as belly breathing, is one of the most common techniques in somatic therapy. By breathing deeply into the diaphragm, you stimulate the **vagus nerve**, which is key to activating the **parasympathetic nervous system**—the part of the body responsible for rest and recovery.

How to Practice Diaphragmatic Breathing

1. Find a comfortable seated or lying position.
2. Place one hand on your chest and the other on your abdomen.
3. Inhale deeply through your nose for a count of four, feeling your abdomen rise as you breathe in.
4. Exhale slowly through your mouth for a count of six, allowing your abdomen to fall.
5. Repeat for several minutes, focusing on the sensation of the breath.

This practice can be done anytime you feel overwhelmed or anxious. Over time, regular breathwork can help to recalibrate your nervous system, making it easier to move out of states of anxiety or distress.

Movement: Releasing Trauma Through the Body

Trauma often leaves us feeling stuck, both emotionally and physically. One of the key principles of somatic therapy is that **movement** can help to release these stuck energies and emotions. When we move our bodies in intentional, mindful ways, we give ourselves the opportunity to process and let go of the trauma that's been stored inside.

Somatic movement doesn't have to be complex—it's not about exercise or fitness but rather about gently moving in ways that feel good and help release tension. This can include simple activities like **stretching**, **shaking**, or even **dancing**.

Example: Mark's Experience with Somatic Movement

Mark, a 50-year-old construction worker, had always been strong and active. After experiencing a traumatic event, he found himself avoiding physical activity and feeling stiff and disconnected from his body. In somatic therapy, his therapist encouraged him to try **shaking**, a technique often used in trauma release. At first, it felt strange, but as Mark let himself shake out his arms, legs, and torso, he began to notice a release of tension he didn't even know he was holding. He described the experience as "freeing," and with regular practice, he began to feel more in tune with his body.

Movement allows trauma survivors to release energy and tension that can become trapped in the body. The key is to move in ways that feel natural and safe, allowing the body to gradually release what it's been holding onto.

Body Scanning: Tuning Into Your Body's Messages

Another foundational technique in somatic therapy is **body scanning**, a practice that involves bringing gentle awareness to different parts of your body, noticing any sensations, tension, or discomfort. This technique helps you become more attuned to your body's needs and can be a powerful tool for releasing stored trauma.

How to Practice a Body Scan

1. Find a quiet, comfortable space where you won't be disturbed.
2. Close your eyes and take a few deep breaths to settle in.
3. Begin by focusing your attention on your toes. Notice any sensations—warmth, tingling, tension—and just observe without judgment.
4. Slowly move your attention up through your legs, abdomen, chest, arms, and head, pausing at each body part to notice what sensations are present.
5. If you encounter areas of tension or discomfort, simply acknowledge them and breathe into them, allowing the body to soften if it feels safe to do so.

Body scanning encourages you to listen to your body's subtle messages. By practicing regularly, you'll begin to notice areas where trauma may be stored and can work towards releasing this tension.

Case Study: Body Scanning in Action

Anna, a 40-year-old lawyer, had always been high-achieving and driven. After a traumatic experience at work, she started experiencing frequent headaches and tightness in her neck and shoulders. She didn't connect these physical symptoms to her trauma until she began body scanning in somatic therapy. As Anna scanned her body, she noticed how tense her shoulders were. By focusing her attention there and gently breathing into the tension, she was able to release it, leading to fewer headaches and a greater sense of emotional relief.

How These Techniques Work Together

While each of these somatic techniques—mindfulness, breathwork, movement, and body scanning—can be practiced individually, they are often most effective when used in combination. For example, you might begin with mindful breathing to calm your nervous system, then move into a body scan to identify areas of tension, followed by gentle movement to release that tension. Over time, these practices help to rewire the body's response to stress and trauma, allowing it to heal and function more effectively. Trauma often disconnects us from our bodies, but through somatic techniques, we can gradually rebuild that connection and restore balance.

Final Thoughts: Reclaiming Your Body's Wisdom

Trauma can make you feel like a stranger in your own body, but somatic techniques offer a pathway back to yourself. These practices are not about forcing change but about **listening** to your body, honoring its signals, and creating space for healing. With patience and compassion, you can learn to release the trauma stored in your body and move towards a life of greater ease, freedom, and connection.

4

The Power of Relationships in Somatic Trauma Therapy

When healing from trauma, relationships are one of the most powerful tools for recovery. Trauma often creates feelings of isolation, disconnection, and mistrust, making it difficult for individuals to feel safe in their bodies or in the world. **Somatic trauma therapy** offers a unique pathway to healing, not just by working with the body, but by emphasizing the importance of **trusting relationships**—whether with a therapist, support group, or loved ones. In this chapter, we'll explore how the therapeutic relationship plays a critical role in the recovery process and how support networks and community involvement can further enhance healing.

Why Relationships Matter in Trauma Recovery

When someone experiences trauma, their ability to feel safe, connected, and supported in relationships is often compromised. Trauma disrupts the body's natural sense of security, causing the nervous system to remain in a state of hypervigilance. In order to heal, it's crucial to restore a sense of safety and trust—and this can't always be done in isolation.

In the context of **somatic trauma therapy**, relationships provide the safety and grounding needed for individuals to access and process their trauma. Trauma is not just an individual experience; it is deeply relational, often originating in interactions with others (e.g., abuse, neglect, violence). Healing, therefore, requires reestablishing **healthy connections** and re-learning how to feel safe with others.

The Therapeutic Relationship: Creating Safety and Trust

The relationship between a client and their somatic therapist is one of the most important factors in the healing process. **Somatic therapists** are trained to help clients feel safe in their bodies and in the therapeutic space. This relationship is built on mutual trust, empathy, and a non-judgmental attitude, allowing the client to explore their trauma without fear.

The therapist's role in **somatic trauma therapy** goes beyond simply guiding physical exercises or mindfulness practices. They are there to help regulate the client's nervous system by providing **attuned presence**, helping the client feel understood, seen, and heard. This process of **co-regulation** allows the client to begin relaxing their body's defenses and to explore the sensations and emotions associated with their trauma.

Sarah, a 28-year-old trauma survivor, came to somatic therapy after years of struggling with anxiety and dissociation. She had difficulty trusting others and often felt disconnected from her body. Her therapist focused on creating a space where Sarah could feel safe—using grounding exercises, gentle touch (with her consent), and validating her experiences.

Over time, Sarah's nervous system began to respond to her therapist's consistent, non-judgmental presence. She learned to trust her therapist, and as a result, she felt more comfortable exploring the physical sensations associated with her trauma. This therapeutic relationship became a cornerstone of Sarah's recovery, allowing her to reclaim her sense of agency and connection.

The Role of Co-Regulation in Healing

Co-regulation is a key concept in somatic trauma therapy. It refers to the way in which one person's nervous system can help regulate another's. When we are in the presence of someone who is calm, empathetic, and attuned to our needs, our own nervous system can begin to relax and shift out of a state of hypervigilance or shutdown.

In trauma survivors, the nervous system often becomes stuck in a state of **dysregulation**—either in **fight/flight** mode (hyperarousal) or **freeze** mode (hypoarousal). A somatic therapist's presence, tone of voice, and body language can provide a calming influence, allowing the client's nervous system to start shifting toward **regulation**.

Example: Co-Regulation in Practice

Imagine a child who falls and scrapes their knee. If the child's caregiver responds with panic, the child is likely to become more upset. However, if the caregiver remains calm and offers comfort, the child can feel safe and begin to regulate their emotions. This same dynamic happens in somatic therapy. The therapist's calm and steady presence helps the client's nervous system downshift from a state of distress to one of **safety and regulation**.

Support Networks: The Power of Connection Beyond Therapy

While the therapeutic relationship is crucial, it's not the only relationship that matters in trauma recovery. A **support network** of trusted friends, family members, or peers can play a significant role in helping someone heal. These relationships provide ongoing emotional support, validation, and a sense of belonging—all of which are essential for restoring safety and connection after trauma.

Trauma survivors often struggle with feelings of isolation and disconnection. By cultivating healthy, supportive relationships, they can begin to rebuild trust in others and the world around them. Support groups, both in-person and online, can also be valuable spaces for trauma survivors to connect with others who share similar experiences.

David, a 40-year-old combat veteran, struggled with post-traumatic stress disorder (PTSD) after returning from deployment. He had difficulty connecting with his family and often felt alone in his experiences. After joining a veterans' support group, David discovered the healing power of peer support. Hearing others share their stories made him feel less isolated, and he began to open up about his own trauma. The group provided a safe, non-judgmental space where David could explore his emotions and experiences.

The relationships David formed in the group, combined with his work in somatic therapy, played a crucial role in his healing journey. He learned that he wasn't alone and that it was possible to rebuild trust and connection with others.

Community: Healing Through Shared Experience

Beyond individual relationships, **community** can also play a vital role in trauma recovery. Being part of a supportive community helps trauma survivors feel connected, valued, and understood. This sense of belonging can be incredibly healing, especially for those who have experienced trauma that involved disconnection from others (such as abuse or neglect).

Community healing initiatives—such as trauma-informed yoga classes, mindfulness groups, or creative arts programs—offer trauma survivors the opportunity to heal in a **collective setting**. These initiatives emphasize the importance of healing as a shared experience, not something that has to be done alone.

Maria, a survivor of domestic abuse, found solace in a community yoga class designed for trauma survivors. The class was held in a safe, welcoming environment where participants could move at their own pace and respect their body's limits. The sense of community in the class helped Maria feel less alone in her healing journey. She found that being surrounded by others who understood her experiences provided a deep sense of connection and validation.

Building a Supportive Healing Network

It's important for trauma survivors to create a **supportive network** that includes not only a therapist but also trusted friends, family members, and community groups. Each relationship in this network plays a different role in the healing process:

- **Therapist**: Provides professional guidance, safety, and co-regulation.
- **Friends and Family**: Offer emotional support, validation, and a sense of belonging.
- **Support Groups**: Provide a space for shared experience and mutual healing.
- **Community**: Creates a broader sense of connection and belonging.

By cultivating a variety of relationships, trauma survivors can ensure that they have the support they need throughout their recovery journey.

At its core, somatic trauma therapy recognizes that healing happens in relationship—both with ourselves and with others. Trauma often leaves us feeling disconnected, but through the power of supportive, trusting relationships, we can begin to rebuild that connection and heal. Whether it's the co-regulation provided by a therapist, the empathy of a friend, or the shared experience of a support group, relationships are essential for trauma recovery.

5

Understanding Trauma and Its Impact: Types of trauma, symptoms, and effects on daily life

Trauma affects individuals in deeply personal ways, reshaping not only their emotional state but also their physical and mental well-being. Understanding trauma requires us to recognize its diverse forms, the complex symptoms that emerge, and the profound influence it can have on every aspect of a person's life. This chapter will guide you through the different types of trauma, common symptoms, and how trauma often ripples into everyday experiences.

What is Trauma?

At its core, trauma is the emotional, physical, and psychological response to highly distressing events. It may result from experiences that overwhelm an individual's ability to cope or integrate the emotions involved. Trauma isn't defined by the event itself but by the way a person responds to that event. For some, an experience might seem manageable, but for others, the same event can be deeply traumatizing, causing lasting emotional scars.

The brain and body respond to trauma as a survival mechanism, activating the fight-or-flight response to protect against danger. When trauma is unresolved, this natural defense can become chronic, leading to prolonged feelings of stress, fear, and tension long after the danger has passed.

Types of Trauma

Not all traumas are the same. They can be categorized into different types based on the nature of the experience and its duration:

- **Acute Trauma**: This form of trauma stems from a single, overwhelming event. Examples include natural disasters, car accidents, or sudden loss. Acute trauma often creates an intense but short-term response, but it can also lead to long-term emotional and psychological issues if not addressed.
- **Chronic Trauma**: Chronic trauma involves repeated or prolonged exposure to distressing experiences. For instance, individuals who endure domestic violence,

bullying, or ongoing medical issues may experience chronic trauma. Unlike acute trauma, chronic trauma tends to embed itself into a person's day-to-day life, making it harder to identify but more persistent.

- **Complex Trauma**: Complex trauma occurs when someone experiences multiple, often interpersonal, traumatic events. This type of trauma typically begins early in life, particularly in the case of childhood neglect, abuse, or dysfunctional family environments. The lasting impact of complex trauma can affect emotional regulation, self-identity, and relationships, with victims often feeling disconnected from their bodies and emotions.

- **Secondary or Vicarious Trauma**: Those who regularly witness or work with individuals suffering from trauma (such as healthcare workers, therapists, or first responders) can experience vicarious trauma. Though they aren't directly impacted, they absorb the emotional weight of others' suffering, leading to symptoms similar to direct trauma.

Symptoms of Trauma

Trauma manifests in a variety of ways, and no two individuals will experience it identically. Here are some of the common symptoms people may face:

- **Physical Symptoms**: Trauma isn't just emotional—it has a significant impact on the body. Many trauma survivors experience chronic pain, headaches, digestive issues, fatigue, and other physical ailments. These symptoms are often linked to the body's stress response being over-activated, keeping the person in a state of hypervigilance. In some cases, people also develop psychosomatic symptoms, where emotional distress triggers physical pain or discomfort.

- **Emotional Symptoms**: Emotional responses to trauma can be both overwhelming and unpredictable. Individuals might feel heightened anxiety, fear, or sadness, or experience outbursts of anger without clear cause. Some trauma survivors may have difficulty regulating their emotions, feeling emotionally "numb" or detached from their feelings as a coping mechanism.

- **Cognitive Symptoms**: Trauma often disrupts thinking patterns. Intrusive memories, flashbacks, and difficulty concentrating are common symptoms. Many trauma survivors struggle with distorted beliefs about themselves or the world, such as feelings of helplessness, guilt, or shame. These cognitive disruptions can make it challenging to maintain a sense of normalcy in everyday activities.

- **Behavioral Symptoms**: Behavioral changes are common among those dealing with trauma. Some may withdraw from relationships, avoid places or situations that remind them of the traumatic event, or engage in self-destructive behaviors like substance abuse. Changes in sleep patterns (such as insomnia or nightmares) and appetite are also common.

Effects of Trauma on Daily Life

Trauma can permeate every corner of an individual's life, leaving them feeling disoriented and disconnected. Here's how trauma affects daily living:

- **Relationships**: Trauma can strain relationships, whether personal, familial, or professional. Survivors often struggle to trust others, fear intimacy, or become isolated as a way of protecting themselves from further harm. On the other end, some individuals may become overly dependent, seeking reassurance or safety from those around them. Family members and friends, too, may struggle to understand the changes in their loved one's behavior, further complicating the dynamic.

- **Work or School**: In the workplace or educational settings, trauma can make it hard to focus or perform tasks. Constant hypervigilance or intrusive thoughts may hinder productivity, while emotional outbursts can damage professional relationships. For students, trauma can affect academic performance, making it difficult to concentrate or retain information. Many trauma survivors report feeling "checked out," unable to stay present in their environment.

- **Physical Health**: The chronic stress response associated with trauma can take a serious toll on physical health. Studies have linked trauma to increased risks for heart disease, obesity, diabetes, and autoimmune disorders. Sleep disorders, such as insomnia or night terrors, further weaken the body's ability to heal and recover.

- **Emotional Well-being**: Trauma deeply influences emotional regulation, often leaving individuals feeling stuck in a loop of fear, sadness, or anger. Unresolved trauma may lead to mental health conditions like post-traumatic stress disorder (PTSD), depression, or anxiety. In many cases, individuals feel disconnected from their emotions and may adopt maladaptive coping strategies, such as self-harm or substance abuse, to deal with overwhelming feelings.

Living with Trauma

Living with trauma can be exhausting, but it's important to remember that healing is possible. Trauma survivors are often incredibly resilient, and with the right support, they can reclaim control over their lives. Recognizing the symptoms and effects of trauma is the first step toward recovery.

Consider the case of Maria, a woman who survived a serious car accident. For years, she lived with chronic anxiety and would avoid driving altogether. Her relationships with her family were strained, as she became withdrawn and irritable, often lashing out over small things. After starting somatic therapy, she learned how trauma had embedded itself in her body—her tension and pain were not just physical but emotional, too. Through simple grounding techniques and gentle movement, Maria began to reconnect with her body, learning to identify and release the stored tension from her trauma. Gradually, her symptoms eased, and she started to reclaim parts of her life she thought were lost forever.

Maria's journey is just one of many. Each individual's experience with trauma is unique, but the path to healing often involves understanding the ways trauma manifests and seeking out practices and relationships that nurture recovery.

6

The Link Between Trauma and Anxiety: How trauma contributes to anxiety and stress

Trauma and anxiety are intimately connected in ways that can be hard to untangle. Trauma doesn't just leave emotional scars; it can fundamentally reshape how we experience the world, influencing how we react to stress and anxiety long after the traumatic event has passed. Many people who have experienced trauma find themselves dealing with heightened anxiety, persistent stress, and an underlying sense of fear that they can't quite explain.

In this chapter, we'll explore how trauma can trigger anxiety, why it makes certain stressors feel overwhelming, and what you can do to begin managing both. We'll walk through the physiological and emotional relationship between trauma and anxiety in a compassionate, easy-to-understand way, using real-life examples to highlight these connections.

Understanding Trauma and Anxiety

To understand the relationship between trauma and anxiety, it's essential to recognize how trauma affects the brain. When we go through a traumatic event, our brain shifts into survival mode. This response is essential when you're in immediate danger—it helps you stay alert, focused, and prepared to protect yourself. The problem arises when the brain gets stuck in this hyper-alert state, even when the threat is no longer present.

The ongoing stress caused by unresolved trauma often turns into anxiety, where the nervous system remains activated even in safe environments. In this heightened state, the brain continues to sense danger, triggering anxiety symptoms that can feel overpowering.

Anxiety and trauma can feed off one another. The initial trauma creates the conditions for heightened anxiety, and over time, the ongoing anxiety can make you feel as if the trauma is still controlling your life. This looping effect keeps many trauma survivors in a cycle of stress and fear, making it hard to regain a sense of control.

How Trauma Triggers Anxiety: The Fight, Flight, and Freeze Response

When the brain detects a threat, it activates the **fight, flight, or freeze** response. This is your body's natural way of preparing to either defend yourself, run from danger, or become still and inconspicuous to avoid harm. For trauma survivors, this response doesn't always turn off when the threat is gone. Instead, the brain may remain locked in a state of heightened alertness, causing long-term anxiety.

For example, imagine you've been in a serious car accident. Even months later, you might feel a surge of anxiety every time you get behind the wheel or even see a car speeding past. Your body reacts as if you're in danger again, even though you're not. This is because your brain associates certain stimuli with the trauma, and your fight-or-flight response is triggered by reminders of the event.

In some cases, trauma survivors may experience the **freeze** response, where the body shuts down emotionally and physically. This response can also cause anxiety, especially in situations where a person feels powerless or trapped. They may feel disconnected, numb, or paralyzed by fear in the face of stress, unable to react as they might normally.

The Body's Response: Why Trauma Makes Us Hypervigilant

Trauma not only affects the brain but also the body. After experiencing trauma, the body can remain in a heightened state of awareness known as **hypervigilance**. This means that even small stressors or reminders of the trauma can trigger an exaggerated response. For many trauma survivors, this looks like constantly scanning their environment for danger, becoming easily startled, or feeling tense and on edge without understanding why.

Hypervigilance is a survival mechanism meant to keep you safe. After a traumatic event, the body learns to remain on high alert, anticipating any future danger. But over time, this constant state of tension becomes exhausting and anxiety-inducing, leaving individuals feeling trapped in their bodies.

Example: Sarah, a trauma survivor, described her experience of hypervigilance after being mugged in her neighborhood. Even in seemingly safe situations, like walking through a well-lit park, she would experience sudden bursts of anxiety, feeling as though someone was following her. Her body would tense, her heart would race, and she would find it difficult to breathe. Even when her rational mind knew she was safe, her body remained convinced that danger was near.

The Role of the Nervous System in Trauma and Anxiety

Your nervous system plays a huge role in how trauma manifests as anxiety. The **autonomic nervous system** regulates bodily functions, including heart rate, digestion, and breathing. It consists of two branches: the **sympathetic nervous system** (which activates the fight-or-flight response) and the **parasympathetic nervous system** (which helps calm the body down after a threat has passed).

For individuals with unresolved trauma, the sympathetic nervous system may be in a constant state of overactivation. This means the fight-or-flight response is triggered more easily, even when no real threat is present. When the parasympathetic system has trouble engaging, it becomes harder for the body to relax, and stress hormones like cortisol and adrenaline remain elevated.

The Vagus Nerve: The vagus nerve, part of the parasympathetic system, plays a crucial role in calming the body after a stress response. It's responsible for regulating many bodily functions, including heart rate, digestion, and mood. Trauma can dysregulate the vagus nerve, making it difficult for individuals to shift from a state of stress back to a relaxed state. This dysregulation often contributes to chronic anxiety, where the body feels stuck in an activated state, unable to rest and recover.

How Trauma and Anxiety Manifest in Daily Life

One of the challenges of trauma-induced anxiety is how it shows up in everyday situations. Trauma survivors often experience a range of anxiety symptoms, from social anxiety to panic attacks, that can severely impact their quality of life.

- **Social Anxiety**: After trauma, interacting with others can feel daunting. Social anxiety is common among trauma survivors, especially if their trauma involved interpersonal relationships or feelings of shame. People may withdraw from social situations, fearing judgment, rejection, or criticism.
- **Panic Attacks**: Panic attacks are intense episodes of fear or anxiety that seem to come out of nowhere. These attacks can be triggered by reminders of trauma or, in some cases, by generalized stress. For trauma survivors, panic attacks may feel like reliving the original event, as the body's stress response takes over completely.
- **Everyday Stressors**: For trauma survivors, even small stressors like a busy workday, a disagreement with a partner, or a delayed appointment can feel overwhelming. Because the body is already on high alert, regular daily stress may feel amplified, contributing to feelings of anxiety and loss of control.

Example: James, a trauma survivor, described how a simple misunderstanding at work would trigger feelings of panic. Even though the situation wasn't inherently dangerous, his body would respond as though he were facing a life-or-death threat. He would feel his heart race, his palms sweat, and his mind go blank, all because his body was conditioned to react this way after years of unresolved trauma.

Healing Trauma-Related Anxiety: A Compassionate Approach

Understanding how trauma contributes to anxiety is the first step in healing. There are several ways individuals can begin to manage trauma-related anxiety, and these approaches often involve working with the body as much as the mind.

- **Somatic Therapy**: Somatic therapies focus on reconnecting the individual to their body, helping them release stored tension and restore a sense of calm. Techniques like grounding exercises, breathwork, and gentle movement can help regulate the nervous system, giving trauma survivors tools to manage their anxiety in the moment.
- **Mindfulness Practices**: Mindfulness is a powerful tool for managing trauma-related anxiety. By becoming aware of your thoughts, feelings, and bodily

sensations in the present moment, you can begin to recognize when anxiety is taking over and practice techniques to bring yourself back to a calm state.

- **Therapeutic Relationships**: A strong, supportive therapeutic relationship can make a significant difference in managing trauma-related anxiety. Therapists who specialize in trauma can help individuals process their experiences in a safe environment and teach techniques for calming the nervous system.

Example: Emily, a woman who had struggled with trauma-related anxiety for years, found relief through a combination of somatic therapy and mindfulness practices. Her therapist taught her grounding techniques that she could use when she felt anxiety rising. Over time, Emily learned how to recognize the early signs of her anxiety and use these tools to bring herself back to the present moment, gradually reducing the frequency of her panic attacks.

II

Foundations of Somatic Trauma Therapy

31

7

Breathing Techniques for Trauma Release: Basic breathing exercises and their benefits

Breathing techniques are foundational tools for trauma recovery, helping regulate emotions and calm the nervous system. Trauma often disrupts normal breathing patterns, leading to shallow, rapid breaths that trigger the body's stress response. Relearning how to breathe deeply and intentionally can release stored trauma and bring the body back to balance.

Why Breathing Matters in Trauma Recovery

Breathing deeply engages the parasympathetic nervous system, helping to calm the body and reduce the fight-or-flight response often triggered by trauma. When practiced regularly, breathing exercises restore a sense of control and safety, grounding trauma survivors in the present moment.

Breathing Techniques for Trauma Release

- 1. **Diaphragmatic Breathing (Belly Breathing)**

How to practice:

- Sit or lie down comfortably.
- Place one hand on your chest and the other on your belly.
- Inhale deeply through your nose, expanding your belly.
- Exhale slowly through your mouth, feeling your belly fall.
- Repeat for 5–10 minutes.

Benefits: Reduces stress, calms the nervous system, and promotes relaxation by allowing deep lung expansion.

- 2. **Box Breathing (Square Breathing)**

How to practice:

- Inhale through your nose for 4 counts.
- Hold your breath for 4 counts.

- Exhale through your mouth for 4 counts.
- Hold for 4 counts.
- Repeat for several cycles.

Benefits: Helps control the body's stress response and promotes emotional regulation.

- 3. **4-7-8 Breathing**

How to practice:

- Inhale through your nose for 4 counts.
- Hold your breath for 7 counts.
- Exhale through your mouth for 8 counts.
- Repeat for 4–8 cycles.

Benefits: Quickly calms the nervous system, reducing anxiety and stress.

- 4. **Alternate Nostril Breathing (Nadi Shodhana)**

How to practice:

- Close your right nostril with your thumb.
- Inhale through your left nostril.
- Close your left nostril with your ring finger, release your right nostril, and exhale.
- Inhale through the right nostril, then exhale through the left.
- Repeat the cycle for 5–10 minutes.

Benefits: Balances the nervous system and helps with emotional clarity.

The Science Behind Breathing and Trauma Release

Breathing exercises activate the **vagus nerve**, which controls the body's relaxation response. Deep, controlled breathing regulates heart rate and lowers cortisol levels, allowing trauma survivors to break the cycle of chronic stress. Regular practice can help trauma survivors regain control of their stress responses, reducing symptoms like anxiety and hypervigilance.

- **How to Integrate Breathing Techniques into Your Daily Life**
- **Start small**: Practice for a few minutes daily, gradually increasing duration.
- **Pair with activities**: Try breathing exercises while commuting or before bed.
- **Use during stress**: Apply these techniques in moments of anxiety to regain calm.

8

Chapter 8

III

10-Minute Daily Exercises for Trauma Recovery

35

9

Week 1-2: Grounding and Safety Exercises

Establishing a Sense of Stability and Security

Grounding techniques are not just simple exercises; they are the foundation upon which trauma recovery rests. By grounding ourselves in the present moment, we begin to regain control over our nervous system, allowing the body to feel safe and at home. Trauma often leaves us feeling disconnected from our bodies, and these exercises will help you re-establish a connection that nurtures feelings of safety and presence.

5-4-3-2-1 Grounding Technique

This sensory-based practice is one of the most effective ways to disrupt intrusive thoughts and anxiety caused by trauma. It's a practical tool you can use anytime, anywhere, to regain control of your body and mind.

- *How it works:* The 5-4-3-2-1 technique uses your five senses to bring attention to your immediate environment. This shifts focus away from distressing memories or anxious thoughts and draws it back into the present.

Instructions:

- Look around and identify **5 things** you can see. Be specific—describe the texture, color, or even the feeling you imagine when you see these objects.
- Identify **4 things** you can touch. Reach out and physically engage with your surroundings, such as the fabric of your clothing, the chair you're sitting on, or the ground beneath your feet.
- Pay attention to **3 sounds** around you, from the hum of a fan to distant conversations.
- Next, focus on **2 smells** you can notice. Even if the smells aren't distinct, imagine the smell of things you associate with comfort (e.g., fresh coffee, a warm meal).

- Finally, identify **1 thing** you can taste. It could be a lingering taste in your mouth or you can sip on water to become aware of the sensation.

This exercise is like hitting the reset button on your nervous system, grounding you back into the safety of the present moment.

Feet-to-Floor Grounding

1. When life feels overwhelming, one of the simplest and most effective ways to ground yourself is by physically reconnecting with the earth beneath you. Trauma can make us feel uprooted, detached, or floating in a state of hyper-vigilance. This exercise helps bring your attention back to your body's direct connection with the ground, enhancing a sense of security.

- ***How it works:***The brain receives sensory input from your feet making contact with the floor, which sends calming signals throughout your body. This brings awareness back to your physical body and disrupts the pattern of trauma-induced hyper-arousal.

Instructions:

- Sit or stand in a comfortable position with both feet firmly on the ground.
- Close your eyes and take several deep breaths, drawing your awareness to the sensation of your feet against the floor.
- Imagine your feet growing roots, sinking deep into the earth, and feeling the support of the ground beneath you. Focus on how stable and strong you are as your feet are planted firmly in the earth.
- Breathe in slowly, holding for a count of 4, and then breathe out for a count of 6. This sends calming signals to your nervous system, reinforcing the feeling of groundedness.

This exercise can be done anywhere—in the middle of a stressful meeting, on public transportation, or at home—providing an immediate anchor to help you feel secure and present.

Safe Space Visualization

1. Our minds are incredibly powerful tools in trauma recovery. Safe space visualization is a tool that creates a mental refuge, a place where you can retreat when life feels too overwhelming. It taps into the body's natural ability to relax

when it feels safe and can serve as a powerful counterbalance to the heightened anxiety caused by trauma.

- ***How it works:***By engaging your imagination, you are able to shift your nervous system from a state of hyper-arousal into one of relaxation. Over time, practicing this visualization can condition your body to feel calm and safe when you revisit this mental refuge.

Instructions:

- Find a quiet and comfortable space where you can sit undisturbed for 5-10 minutes.
- Close your eyes and take several deep, calming breaths.
- Begin to visualize a place where you feel completely safe. It can be a real place—like a beach, forest, or childhood home—or an imaginary one. Focus on engaging all of your senses: What do you see? What do you hear? Can you feel a breeze on your skin or the warmth of the sun?
- Stay in this mental space for as long as you need, revisiting it throughout the day if stress or anxiety begins to build.

This practice can be a lifeline for those who feel unsafe in their daily life. It acts as a mental sanctuary, helping you build resilience against the ongoing challenges of trauma recovery.

Why Grounding is Essential in the Early Stages of Trauma Recovery

At the heart of trauma recovery is the need to establish safety. Grounding techniques like the ones described here are critical because they tap into the body's inherent wisdom. These practices help shift the autonomic nervous system away from a fight-or-flight response and into a parasympathetic state, where healing can truly begin. Without this initial foundation of safety, the body will continue to operate in survival mode, which prevents deeper emotional healing.

Daily Practice Tip:

Consistency is key. Trauma recovery is not a quick fix, but a gradual reestablishment of trust within your own body. Incorporate these grounding exercises into your daily routine—

set aside time each morning or before bed to check in with your body. Over time, these practices will become second nature, making it easier for you to find calm amidst the chaos.

10

Week 3-4: Release and Let Go Exercises

As you move through your trauma recovery journey, it becomes essential to release the physical tension your body holds onto. These exercises focus on loosening the grip of trauma-induced stress and creating space for relaxation and renewal. Trauma often manifests as tightness or stiffness in the body, and through these practices, we can create a pathway to deeper emotional and physical release.

Progressive Muscle Relaxation (PMR)

Progressive Muscle Relaxation is a tried-and-true method for releasing built-up tension in the body. Trauma often causes certain muscles to stay in a state of hyperarousal, creating tightness and discomfort. By tensing and then consciously releasing each muscle group, you can reprogram your body to relax deeply.

- *How it works*: PMR teaches your body how to distinguish between tension and relaxation, helping you become aware of any areas holding onto stress.

Instructions:

- Start by sitting or lying down in a comfortable position. Close your eyes and take a few deep breaths.
- Begin with your feet—tense the muscles for 5-7 seconds, really focusing on the sensation of tightness.
- Then, slowly exhale and release the tension, allowing your muscles to completely relax. Notice how the release feels in contrast to the tension.
- Gradually move up your body: legs, abdomen, chest, hands, arms, neck, and finally, your face. After completing each muscle group, enjoy the overall feeling of relaxation.
- As you progress, notice any specific areas that hold more tension and practice releasing them consciously.

Practicing PMR regularly teaches your body how to relax more quickly in moments of stress and can be a powerful tool for trauma recovery.

Breath and Sigh Technique

Breathing is one of the most immediate ways to calm your nervous system, but many people overlook the therapeutic power of the sigh. This technique helps release emotional and physical tension from the chest, where trauma often causes tightness or discomfort.

- ***How it works****:* The act of intentionally sighing allows your diaphragm to fully engage, helping release tension not just in the chest but also in the neck, shoulders, and upper body.

Instructions:

- Sit or stand comfortably. Inhale deeply through your nose, filling your lungs completely.
- As you exhale, let out a deep, audible sigh. Allow your shoulders to drop and notice the tension leaving your body.
- Repeat this process 5 times, paying attention to the sensation of letting go with each exhale.
- If any emotions arise during the sigh, allow them to come up without judgment. This is your body's way of releasing built-up stress and trauma.
- You can do this exercise throughout the day, especially when you feel emotionally overwhelmed or physically tight.

This exercise is deceptively simple but profoundly effective. The more you practice, the more it becomes a reliable tool for quickly releasing tension in stressful moments.

Shaking for Tension Release

Shaking is a primal and natural way to release trauma that is often stored as energy in the body. Animals in the wild instinctively shake after experiencing a stressful event, but humans tend to suppress this impulse. By deliberately engaging in shaking, we allow our bodies to discharge pent-up energy, leaving us feeling lighter and more relaxed.

- ***How it works****:* Shaking acts as a reset for the nervous system, encouraging the release of trauma-stored energy that can manifest as muscle tightness, anxiety, or hypervigilance.

Instructions:

- Stand in an open space with your feet hip-width apart.
- Start by gently shaking your arms, legs, and torso. You can begin slowly, gradually increasing the intensity as you feel comfortable.
- Let your body shake freely, without controlling the movement. Focus on the sensation of energy being released as you shake out any tightness or stiffness in your muscles.
- After 1-2 minutes, slow down the shaking and return to a still position. Take a few deep breaths, noticing how your body feels after the release.
- This can be repeated daily, especially after experiencing a stressful or emotionally charged situation.

This technique can feel unfamiliar at first, but it's one of the most effective ways to physically release trauma from your body. The more you practice, the more natural it becomes to use shaking as a tool for relief.

Why Releasing Tension is Essential for Trauma Recovery

Trauma creates deep-rooted patterns of holding—whether it's tight shoulders, clenched jaws, or tension in the chest. If we don't actively work to release these patterns, they can build up over time, leading to chronic pain, stress, and emotional blockages. These exercises offer a pathway to unwind that tension and promote healing on a deeper level.

Daily Practice Tip:

Set aside a few minutes each day to engage in one or more of these exercises. Releasing tension is not a one-time event, but a practice that gradually loosens the grip trauma holds on your body. Over time, you'll find it easier to relax, even in situations that used to trigger anxiety or stress.

11

Week 5-6: Emotional Regulation Exercises (Building Emotional Resilience and Awareness)

During trauma recovery, intense emotions can emerge unpredictably. The goal of these exercises is to cultivate emotional regulation, enabling you to process and respond to difficult emotions with awareness and self-compassion. By developing these skills, you strengthen your emotional resilience and become more attuned to your emotional landscape.

The Body Scan for Emotional Awareness

The body often stores emotional tension in specific areas, such as the chest, abdomen, or shoulders. A body scan helps you locate and release these pockets of tension, improving emotional awareness and fostering relaxation. This exercise brings attention to the physical sensations associated with emotions, allowing you to identify and release stored stress or discomfort.

- *How it works:* The body scan promotes a nonjudgmental awareness of where emotions may be held, providing a gentle way to release tension. It's a useful tool to check in with yourself daily.

Instructions:

- Find a quiet space where you can sit or lie down comfortably.
- Close your eyes and take a few deep breaths to center yourself.
- Start at the top of your head and slowly scan downward, paying attention to each part of your body. Notice any areas of tightness, discomfort, or tension.
- As you identify these areas, breathe deeply and imagine the tension melting away with each exhale.
- If emotions arise during the scan, allow them to surface without judgment, and continue to focus on releasing physical tension.

This exercise helps foster a deeper connection between your body and emotions, building awareness of how trauma manifests physically and emotionally.

The 4-7-8 Breath for Calm

This breathing technique is an effective way to calm your nervous system when you feel overwhelmed by emotions or stress. By controlling the breath, you can activate the parasympathetic nervous system, which helps bring a sense of calm and relaxation.

- ***How it works:*** The 4-7-8 breath helps manage emotional overwhelm by slowing down your breathing and promoting mindfulness. It is especially useful during moments of anxiety or heightened stress.

Instructions:

- Sit in a comfortable position with your back straight.
- Inhale through your nose quietly for a count of 4 seconds.
- Hold your breath for a count of 7 seconds, allowing your body to pause and relax.
- Slowly exhale through your mouth for a count of 8 seconds, fully emptying your lungs.
- Repeat this cycle 5-7 times, focusing on the soothing rhythm of your breath.

This technique is a powerful yet simple tool to regulate emotions, making it easier to regain control during difficult moments.

Name, Pause, Breathe

Emotional regulation starts with awareness. This exercise helps you acknowledge and name strong emotions as they arise, creating a healthy separation between you and the emotion. By naming your emotion, you reduce its intensity and allow yourself the space to respond thoughtfully.

- ***How it works:*** Naming an emotion gives you control over it, making it less overwhelming. Pausing creates a moment of reflection, and breathing restores calm. This combination encourages emotional resilience and a mindful response to emotional triggers.

Instructions:

- When a strong emotion surfaces (e.g., anger, sadness, fear), take a moment to name it aloud or silently. For example, say, "I feel angry" or "I feel anxious."
- After naming it, pause and reflect on what you're feeling. Instead of reacting, give yourself space to observe the emotion.
- Take three deep breaths, allowing each exhale to soften the intensity of the emotion.
- As you breathe, notice how naming and acknowledging the emotion creates a sense of calm and control.

This exercise can be used anytime, anywhere, and is a simple way to interrupt emotional reactivity and foster healthier emotional responses.

Why Emotional Regulation is Crucial for Trauma Recovery

Emotions play a significant role in trauma recovery. Often, individuals feel overwhelmed by emotions they cannot fully process or understand. By practicing emotional regulation techniques, you strengthen your emotional awareness, helping you to navigate difficult moments with more ease and control. These exercises are tools that help build resilience, ensuring that intense emotions don't overpower your sense of safety and well-being.

Daily Practice Tip:

Integrate emotional regulation exercises into your daily routine. Whether it's a body scan in the morning, breathwork during moments of stress, or naming emotions as they arise throughout the day, these tools help manage the emotional waves that often accompany trauma recovery. Over time, you'll find that these practices make it easier to stay present, calm, and emotionally grounded in difficult situations.

12

Quick Somatic Exercises for Trauma Release: 10-Minute Daily Routines for Beginners

Trauma recovery doesn't always require long, drawn-out practices. These quick somatic routines can be seamlessly integrated into your daily life, whether you're at home, work, or even on the move. Designed for beginners, these 10-minute exercises are powerful yet simple, helping to promote calm, release stored tension, and support ongoing healing.

Box Breathing for Instant Calm

1. Breathing is one of the quickest and most effective ways to regulate your nervous system. Box breathing, also known as square breathing, is a mindful technique that balances your breath, reduces stress, and centers your focus. It's a powerful tool in moments of anxiety or emotional overwhelm.

- ***How it works:***By slowing down your breath and creating a rhythmic pattern, box breathing engages the parasympathetic nervous system, which helps reduce the fight-or-flight response.

Instructions:

- Inhale deeply through your nose for 4 counts, focusing on filling your lungs.
- Hold your breath for 4 counts, allowing your body to pause in stillness.
- Slowly exhale for 4 counts, releasing any tension or stress.
- Hold again for 4 counts before starting the next breath.
- Repeat this cycle for 10 minutes, maintaining focus on the rhythm of your breath and noticing how your body begins to relax.

Box breathing is effective not only in managing stress but also in creating a moment of mindfulness, helping you reconnect with your body and reduce tension.

Body Tapping for Energy Release

1. Body tapping, also known as emotional freedom technique (EFT), is a simple way to stimulate energy flow and release stored emotional or physical tension. It encourages circulation and helps reawaken your body's natural rhythms, providing relief from trauma-induced stress and lethargy.

- ***How it works:***Body tapping lightly activates the meridian points in your body, similar to acupuncture, but without the need for needles. By tapping specific areas, you stimulate energy flow and allow tension to dissipate.

Instructions:

- Start at your head and gently tap with your fingertips, working your way down to your chest, arms, and legs.
- Focus on areas where you feel tension or tightness.
- Tap gently but rhythmically, paying attention to the sensation in each area.
- As you work from head to toe, breathe deeply and imagine any stored tension being released with each tap.
- Continue for 5-10 minutes, then take a moment to feel the subtle energy shift in your body.

This exercise is perfect when you need to quickly recharge or shake off lingering tension, making it a practical tool for busy days.

Butterfly Hug for Self-Soothing

1. The butterfly hug is a gentle, self-soothing technique that helps calm your nervous system and foster a sense of safety. Often used in trauma therapy, it's a powerful tool to use when you feel triggered or anxious. This exercise is simple, discreet, and can be practiced anytime, anywhere.

- ***How it works:*** By crossing your arms over your chest and creating a tapping rhythm, the butterfly hug stimulates bilateral stimulation, which helps process emotions and reduce feelings of distress. It creates a comforting, safe sensation in your body.

Instructions:

- Sit or stand in a comfortable position.
- Cross your arms over your chest, placing your hands on opposite shoulders.
- Begin tapping your shoulders gently, alternating between left and right.
- As you tap, breathe deeply and focus on the soothing rhythm.
- You can repeat affirmations like "I am safe" or "I am grounded" while doing this exercise.
- Continue for 5-10 minutes, allowing yourself to fully relax into the rhythm and the comfort it brings.

This exercise is ideal when you need to quickly calm down and reconnect with a sense of inner safety. It's especially effective during moments of high anxiety or emotional overwhelm.

Why These Quick Somatic Exercises Work

The body and mind are deeply interconnected. These somatic exercises help regulate the nervous system, discharge stored tension, and create a sense of grounding and safety, essential for trauma recovery. The beauty of these routines lies in their simplicity—you can incorporate them into your day no matter where you are or how busy your schedule is. With consistent practice, they provide relief from stress and trauma-related symptoms while promoting emotional resilience.

Pro Tip for Consistency:

Choose one exercise to practice at the same time each day. This helps build a routine and allows you to deepen your experience with the technique, making it easier to call upon in moments of need.

IV

Emotional Regulation and Self-Compassion

49

13

Emotional Regulation with Somatic Techniques: Identifying and releasing stored emotions

In trauma recovery, emotional regulation is vital for managing overwhelming feelings and fostering resilience. Somatic techniques offer powerful methods to identify and release emotions that are stored in the body, helping to ease emotional tension and foster healing.

Body Scan for Emotional Awareness

1. This technique promotes self-awareness by helping you locate and address areas where emotions may be trapped within your body. As you scan from head to toe, you can identify physical manifestations of emotions—such as tightness or discomfort—and use deep breathing to release the tension.

Instructions:

- Find a quiet, comfortable space and close your eyes.
- Begin scanning your body slowly, starting from your head and moving toward your feet.
- Pay attention to areas of tension or unease. For example, you might notice tightness in your chest when feeling sadness, or tension in your jaw from frustration.
- As you become aware of these areas, breathe deeply and focus on releasing the tension with each exhale. Visualize the emotional tightness dissolving.
- This practice can take 5-10 minutes and is especially effective for emotional grounding and awareness.

The 4-7-8 Breathing for Emotional Stability

1. The 4-7-8 breathing technique is a simple but powerful method to calm the nervous system during moments of emotional overwhelm. It slows down your breathing pattern, allowing the body to shift from a state of heightened arousal to one of relaxation.

- ***Instructions***:
- Inhale through your nose for 4 seconds.
- Hold your breath for 7 seconds, creating a brief pause to cultivate stillness.
- Exhale through your mouth for 8 seconds, releasing any emotional tension with the out-breath.
- Repeat the process for 5-7 cycles, observing how your body gradually relaxes. This method is particularly useful when feeling anxious, angry, or emotionally flooded.

The "Name, Pause, Breathe" Technique

1. Emotions can sometimes feel overwhelming and hard to manage. The "Name, Pause, Breathe" technique teaches you to create space between yourself and your emotions, helping you respond rather than react.

- ***Instructions***:
- When a strong emotion surfaces, acknowledge it by naming it aloud or in your mind ("I feel anxious," "I feel frustrated").
- Pause for a moment without judgment. Allow yourself to sit with the emotion rather than immediately acting on it.
- Take three deep breaths, focusing on the rise and fall of your chest. This helps shift your emotional state and allows for greater clarity.
- By simply naming the emotion and taking a breath, you give yourself control over your reactions, fostering emotional regulation.

Why Somatic Techniques Work for Emotional Regulation

Emotions, especially those tied to trauma, often manifest physically. Somatic techniques create a bridge between body and mind, allowing individuals to process feelings in a more grounded and embodied way. By practicing body awareness, mindful breathing, and acknowledging emotions without judgment, you build a stronger capacity to manage difficult emotions, creating a more stable and regulated emotional state.

14

Techniques for processing fear, anger, and sadness

Emotions like fear, anger, and sadness are fundamental human experiences, and somatic techniques can offer powerful ways to process these emotions. Below are some specific techniques for each emotion:

Processing Fear

Fear often manifests as tightness in the chest, a racing heart, or shallow breathing. To process fear, grounding exercises like **Box Breathing** and **Feet-to-Floor Grounding** are effective. These techniques help calm the nervous system by anchoring your awareness in the present moment.

- **Box Breathing**: Inhale for 4 seconds, hold for 4, exhale for 4, and hold for 4. Repeat this for several minutes.
- **Feet-to-Floor Grounding**: Sit with both feet on the ground, feel the support of the earth, and breathe deeply, focusing on the connection with the ground. This technique restores a sense of stability.

Processing Anger

Anger is often stored in the body as tension in the jaw, fists, or upper body. Releasing this pent-up energy through physical movement is key to processing anger. Somatic techniques like **Progressive Muscle Relaxation** or **Shaking** help release the muscular tension associated with anger.

- **Progressive Muscle Relaxation**: Tense and then release each muscle group, moving from the feet to the head. This releases built-up anger stored in the body.
- **Shaking**: Stand with feet hip-width apart, and gently shake your arms, legs, and body. Gradually increase the intensity, letting your body move freely until the anger is released.

Processing Sadness

Sadness often creates a sense of heaviness or tightness in the chest and throat. Processing sadness through somatic techniques involves acknowledging the emotion and allowing its release in a safe, controlled manner. Practices like **Breath and Sigh** and **Butterfly Hug** are helpful for this.

- **Breath and Sigh**: Take a deep breath in and exhale with a sigh, releasing the tension from your chest and throat.
- **Butterfly Hug**: Cross your arms over your chest, with hands on your shoulders, and gently tap alternately while taking deep breaths. This self-soothing technique helps process sadness by promoting safety and calm.

Integrating Emotional Processing into Daily Life

The key to effectively managing fear, anger, and sadness is consistency. Regular practice of these somatic techniques helps individuals develop emotional resilience over time. Whether used in moments of emotional overwhelm or as part of a daily routine, these techniques empower individuals to process and release their emotions in a healthy, embodied way.

15

The Role of Self-Compassion in Healing: Practicing kindness and understanding during recovery

Self-compassion is the practice of treating yourself with the same kindness, understanding, and care that you would offer to a close friend during moments of struggle. In trauma recovery, self-compassion is essential as it counters feelings of shame, guilt, and self-judgment—emotions that often impede healing.

Trauma can leave individuals feeling unworthy, broken, or somehow responsible for their pain. These beliefs create a cycle of self-blame, which can prevent people from fully engaging with the healing process. However, cultivating self-compassion interrupts this cycle and creates an internal environment where healing is more likely to occur.

Dr. Kristin Neff, a leading researcher on self-compassion, identifies three core components:

- **Self-Kindness**: Being warm and understanding towards ourselves when we suffer, fail, or feel inadequate.
- **Common Humanity**: Recognizing that suffering is a shared human experience, not something we go through alone.
- **Mindfulness**: Holding our painful thoughts and emotions in balanced awareness rather than ignoring them or becoming consumed by them.

How Self-Compassion Supports Healing

- **Counteracting Shame and Self-Blame**: Trauma survivors often struggle with intense feelings of shame and guilt. Self-compassion offers an alternative narrative, one that acknowledges suffering without assigning blame. For instance, rather than thinking, "I'm weak for feeling this way," self-compassion reframes it as, "It's human to feel vulnerable after what I've been through."

- **Emotional Resilience**: By practicing self-compassion, individuals build emotional resilience, allowing them to face painful memories and emotions without becoming overwhelmed. This resilience is crucial for trauma recovery, as it supports a gentle and patient approach to processing difficult emotions.
- **Promoting Self-Acceptance**: Trauma survivors often feel disconnected from their bodies and emotions, perceiving them as foreign or untrustworthy. Self-compassion fosters self-acceptance, encouraging individuals to embrace their bodies, emotions, and experiences as parts of their journey, not as enemies to overcome.

Practices for Cultivating Self-Compassion

1. **Loving-Kindness Meditation**: This meditation practice involves sending well-wishes to yourself and others. Begin by saying phrases like, "May I be happy, may I be healthy, may I be safe," and gradually extend those wishes to others in your life. This practice nurtures feelings of warmth and empathy, reducing self-criticism.
2. **The Self-Compassion Break**: During moments of intense self-judgment or stress, pause and acknowledge your suffering. Place a hand over your heart and say, "This is a moment of suffering. Suffering is a part of life. May I be kind to myself in this moment." This short exercise helps shift your mindset from self-criticism to self-care.
3. **Writing a Self-Compassionate Letter**: Write a letter to yourself as if you were writing to a dear friend going through a similar experience. Offer words of comfort, understanding, and encouragement. This exercise can help shift your inner dialogue to one that is more compassionate and supportive.

Integrating Self-Compassion into Daily Life

- **Start Small**: Self-compassion doesn't require grand gestures. It could be as simple as taking a deep breath when you're feeling overwhelmed or giving yourself permission to rest when you're tired. Small acts of kindness towards yourself can add up over time and become a part of your regular routine.
- **Mindful Self-Awareness**: Practice being aware of your thoughts and feelings without judgment. For example, if you notice you're being critical of yourself, take a step back and say, "I'm having the thought that I'm not good enough right

now." By observing your thoughts rather than identifying with them, you create space for self-compassion to grow.

- **Challenge Self-Critical Thoughts**: Whenever a self-critical thought arises, ask yourself, "Would I say this to a friend going through something similar?" If the answer is no, reframe the thought with more kindness and understanding.

Self-Compassion and Somatic Healing

Self-compassion can also play a significant role in somatic healing by helping individuals reconnect with their bodies in a gentle and caring way. Many trauma survivors experience feelings of disconnection or distrust towards their bodies due to past trauma. Somatic techniques combined with self-compassion allow survivors to reclaim a sense of safety and trust in their bodies, helping them navigate the emotional and physical sensations associated with trauma.

For example, a survivor practicing **Body Scan Meditation** can approach areas of discomfort or tension with curiosity and kindness rather than frustration. Instead of focusing on what is "wrong" with their body, they can cultivate an attitude of care: "This tension is here for a reason, and I'm going to gently listen to what it needs."

In **Grounding Exercises**, when fear or anxiety arises, self-compassion encourages an individual to stay present with their experience without judgment. If grounding feels difficult, they might tell themselves, "It's okay that this feels hard right now. I'm doing my best, and that's enough."

16

Letting Go of Shame and Guilt - Embracing vulnerability for true healing

Shame and guilt often bind individuals to their trauma, creating emotional barriers that hinder healing. Letting go of these emotions requires acknowledging the pain, embracing vulnerability, and fostering self-acceptance.

Understanding the Roots of Shame and Guilt

Trauma survivors often internalize their experiences, leading to deep feelings of shame ("I am bad") and guilt ("I did something wrong"). These emotions can become overwhelming, convincing survivors that they deserved the trauma or are somehow responsible for it. This cycle reinforces self-blame, stifling the healing process. Understanding that these emotions are natural but not necessarily accurate representations of reality is the first step towards letting them go.

The Power of Vulnerability

Vulnerability, though often perceived as weakness, is a courageous act in the context of trauma recovery. It allows individuals to confront their emotions rather than suppress them. By embracing vulnerability, survivors create space for authentic emotional expression, making room for healing. Dr. Brené Brown, a prominent researcher on vulnerability, emphasizes that vulnerability is not about exposing ourselves indiscriminately but about taking measured risks to show up fully, even when the outcome is uncertain.

Steps to Letting Go of Shame and Guilt

1. **Acknowledge and Name the Emotions**: The first step towards healing is recognizing and naming the shame and guilt. Say aloud or write down, "I feel ashamed because…" or "I feel guilty because…". By naming the emotions, you bring them into the light, making them easier to address.

2. **Challenge the Narrative**: Often, shame and guilt stem from faulty beliefs. Ask yourself, "Am I really responsible for this?" or "Would I blame someone else in my position?" This helps create distance between yourself and the overwhelming emotions, allowing for a more objective perspective.

3. **Reframe the Story**: Instead of focusing on self-blame, try reframing your experience through a compassionate lens. For example, rather than thinking, "I should have done something differently," say, "I did the best I could with the information and resources I had at the time."

4. **Practice Self-Compassion**: Engage in practices like loving-kindness meditation or self-compassionate journaling to foster a kinder inner dialogue. Remind yourself that making mistakes or experiencing trauma does not define your worth.

5. **Embrace Your Imperfections**: Let go of the belief that you need to be perfect to be deserving of healing. Accepting your imperfections and vulnerabilities allows you to heal in an authentic way, free from the weight of unrealistic expectations.

6. **Share Your Story**: While vulnerability must be carefully managed, sharing your story in safe spaces can lift the burden of shame. Whether it's with a trusted friend, therapist, or support group, expressing your experiences helps break the isolation shame thrives on.

7. **Release Through Somatic Practices**: Since trauma is often stored in the body, somatic techniques like breathwork, body scanning, and grounding can help release the physical tension associated with shame and guilt. Movement-based therapies, such as yoga or dance, also offer a way to let go of stored emotional energy.

Why Letting Go of Shame and Guilt is Crucial for Healing

Shame and guilt perpetuate the trauma cycle by keeping survivors stuck in the past. Letting go of these emotions allows for greater self-forgiveness and the ability to move forward. Healing comes when individuals can look at their trauma without judgment, recognizing that they are not defined by their worst moments but by their resilience and capacity for growth.

Building New Narratives

Letting go of shame and guilt does not mean forgetting the trauma but rather reframing the experience. Survivors can reclaim their power by building a new narrative—one that honors their pain but also celebrates their strength and survival. As the story changes, so does the individual's relationship with their trauma.

The Role of Community in Letting Go

Healing shame and guilt often requires the presence of others. Trauma isolates, while healing connects. Supportive communities—whether in the form of friends, family, therapists, or fellow survivors—provide the validation and empathy necessary to release self-blame. In these safe spaces, vulnerability is not a risk but a pathway to healing.

V

Advanced Techniques and Specialized Applications

17

Somatic Trauma Therapy for Specific Traumas: PTSD, complex trauma, and attachment trauma

PTSD: Somatic Grounding and Pendulation

1. **Pendulation Technique**:

- This technique helps manage the overwhelming sensations that often accompany PTSD.
- **Instructions**: Begin by focusing on areas of tension or discomfort in your body, noticing the sensations without judgment. Then, shift your attention to a part of your body that feels neutral or relaxed. Alternate between these two areas in cycles of 20–30 seconds. The pendulation technique allows the nervous system to slowly process intense emotions without becoming overwhelmed, facilitating a sense of calm. Over time, this practice trains your system to move between states of stress and relaxation with greater ease.

1. **Body Boundary Exercise**:

- Individuals with PTSD often struggle with feeling safe in their body. This exercise helps them reestablish a connection to their physical boundaries and a sense of control.
- **Instructions**: Stand or sit comfortably, and close your eyes. Visualize an energetic boundary extending a few inches away from your skin, like a protective bubble. Slowly and mindfully run your hands along this imagined boundary, noting any sensations of safety or discomfort. Practice creating and reinforcing this boundary regularly. Over time, this can help reestablish a sense of personal space and safety within your body.

Complex Trauma: Somatic Tracking and Gradual Exposure

1. **Somatic Tracking**:

- Complex trauma often results in dissociation or avoidance of bodily sensations. Somatic tracking helps reintegrate awareness of physical sensations without judgment or fear.

- **Instructions**: Begin by sitting quietly in a safe space. Close your eyes and take several deep breaths. Shift your focus to your body, noticing areas of tension, discomfort, or numbness. Avoid the urge to change or control these sensations—simply observe them. After 2–3 minutes, switch to a part of the body that feels more at ease. This technique helps expand the capacity to experience distress without dissociating and builds tolerance for processing unresolved trauma.

1. **Gradual Exposure to Sensation**:

- For those with complex trauma, certain bodily sensations may trigger flashbacks or emotional overwhelm. Gradual exposure to these sensations can help release stored trauma.

- **Instructions**: Identify a sensation in your body that feels overwhelming (e.g., tightness in the chest). Spend a few moments acknowledging the sensation without judgment. Now, introduce a grounding element such as gentle breathing or visualizing a safe place. Practice staying with the sensation while using grounding techniques to prevent emotional flooding. Over time, your ability to stay with difficult sensations will increase, aiding trauma resolution.

Attachment Trauma: Safe-Touch Exercises and Embodied Relational Repair

1. **Safe-Touch Grounding**:

- Attachment trauma often manifests as difficulties with feeling safe, either alone or with others. Safe-touch grounding allows individuals to provide self-comfort through the body.

- **Instructions**: Find a soft object (like a pillow or blanket) and hold it close to your chest while sitting or lying down. Apply gentle pressure with your hands, noticing how the softness feels against your body. Take deep breaths and focus on the soothing sensation of holding something close. This exercise nurtures feelings of safety and self-compassion, gradually healing attachment wounds.

1. **Embodied Relational Repair**:

- Attachment trauma may stem from inconsistent or unsafe relational dynamics. This exercise can help individuals rebuild their capacity for trust and connection.

- **Instructions**: Sit across from a trusted partner or therapist. Begin by making gentle eye contact, then practice mirroring each other's breathing rhythm. After a few moments, experiment with physical gestures like holding hands or lightly touching the arm. Focus on the sensations in your body during this interaction, especially any feelings of comfort, fear, or vulnerability. Over time, this somatic connection fosters trust, emotional attunement, and relational healing.

These advanced practices cater to the specific needs of PTSD, complex trauma, and attachment trauma by addressing the body's stored responses. They help individuals reconnect with their body in safe, measured ways that promote long-term healing and recovery.

63

18

Integrating Somatic Trauma Therapy with Cognitive-Behavioral Therapy (CBT), Mindfulness, and Meditation

Why Combine Therapies?

Trauma is a multifaceted experience that affects both the mind and body. While somatic trauma therapy addresses the physical and emotional imprints of trauma stored in the body, integrating it with cognitive-behavioral therapy (CBT), mindfulness, and meditation creates a more holistic approach to healing. These complementary therapies target different aspects of trauma, promoting overall emotional resilience, regulation, and long-term recovery. This chapter explores how combining these techniques enhances therapeutic outcomes and provides individuals with a robust toolkit for healing.

Cognitive-Behavioral Therapy and Somatic Trauma Therapy

CBT focuses on changing unhelpful cognitive patterns that arise after trauma, such as intrusive thoughts or negative self-beliefs. However, trauma also lives in the body, and that's where somatic trauma therapy comes in. By blending both approaches, individuals can address cognitive distortions **and** the physical sensations associated with trauma.

1. Anchoring Cognitive Work with Somatic Awareness

Cognitive processing becomes more effective when paired with somatic awareness techniques. For example, while engaging in CBT exercises to challenge negative thoughts, individuals can use grounding techniques to stay present and connected to their bodies, preventing emotional overwhelm.

Example Exercise: Cognitive Grounding Combo

- **Step 1**: During a CBT session, when a difficult emotion arises (e.g., fear), pause and practice a grounding exercise such as placing both feet firmly on the ground.
- **Step 2**: As you explore the thought triggering the emotion (e.g., "I'm not safe"), take deep belly breaths and notice any sensations in your body. This links

cognitive awareness with physical sensations, creating a dual focus that helps regulate emotional responses.

2. Using Body-Based Practices to Break Cognitive Loops

Trauma survivors often experience thought loops (e.g., ruminations or flashbacks). By adding somatic techniques, individuals can break these loops by shifting attention away from the thoughts and into the body.

Example Practice: Thought-Body Disruption

- **Step 1**: When a distressing thought arises, identify where you feel it in your body (e.g., tightness in the chest).
- **Step 2**: Use a somatic release exercise like shaking out your arms or doing a quick, intentional movement to disrupt the cognitive loop. By engaging your body, you bring yourself out of your mind and into the present moment.

Mindfulness and Somatic Trauma Therapy

Mindfulness involves non-judgmental awareness of the present moment, helping individuals stay grounded and connected. When combined with somatic therapy, mindfulness enhances body awareness, making it easier to detect early signs of distress or emotional triggers before they become overwhelming.

1. Mindful Body Scanning

Body scanning is a powerful tool in both mindfulness and somatic therapy. It allows individuals to tune into the body's sensations, identifying areas of tension or discomfort that may be linked to trauma.

Example Exercise: Mindful Body Scan

- **Step 1**: Find a quiet space to sit or lie down comfortably. Close your eyes and take a few deep breaths.
- **Step 2**: Slowly scan your body from head to toe, noticing sensations such as tightness, heat, or discomfort.
- **Step 3**: As you identify areas of tension, breathe into them, releasing judgment. Just observe the sensations as they shift or release.
- **Benefit**: Regular practice helps you stay attuned to your body's needs and manage trauma responses with greater ease.

2. Mindful Movement

Incorporating movement into mindfulness practices bridges the gap between cognitive awareness and physical healing. Gentle movements, such as yoga or tai chi, promote flexibility, grounding, and calmness while providing an outlet for stored trauma energy.

Example Practice: Mindful Walking

- **Step 1**: Go for a slow, mindful walk, paying attention to each step. Feel the ground beneath your feet.
- **Step 2**: Focus on your breath as you walk, noticing the rhythm of your steps and the way your body feels as you move.
- **Benefit**: Mindful walking can reduce anxiety, help process emotions, and promote grounding during emotional distress.

Meditation and Somatic Trauma Therapy

Meditation, especially trauma-sensitive forms, helps regulate the nervous system and fosters a deep sense of calm. Combining somatic practices with meditation supports trauma recovery by promoting long-term regulation of the autonomic nervous system, which is often disrupted by trauma.

1. Trauma-Sensitive Meditation

Unlike traditional meditation practices that may encourage stillness and silence, trauma-sensitive meditation incorporates gentle somatic techniques to avoid triggering overwhelm.

Example Practice: Trauma-Sensitive Breath Meditation

- **Step 1**: Sit comfortably and begin by placing your hands on your belly. Close your eyes and inhale deeply through your nose, feeling your belly expand.
- **Step 2**: As you exhale, release tension in your shoulders, neck, and jaw. Focus on your breath and its calming rhythm.
- **Step 3**: If distressing thoughts or sensations arise, gently open your eyes and ground yourself by focusing on a nearby object or feeling your feet on the floor.
- **Benefit**: This practice allows you to stay connected to your body while maintaining a calm, meditative state.

2. Somatic Visualization for Emotional Release

Incorporating visualization into meditation can support the release of stored trauma by engaging the imagination to process emotions and trauma.

Example Practice: Safe Space Visualization

- **Step 1**: Sit in a quiet space, close your eyes, and begin deep, rhythmic breathing.
- **Step 2**: Visualize a safe, calming environment—perhaps a forest, beach, or peaceful room. Imagine every detail, including sights, sounds, and smells.
- **Step 3**: As you relax into this space, imagine releasing your fears, worries, or pain into the environment around you, letting it dissolve as you breathe deeply.

- **Benefit**: This exercise promotes emotional release in a way that feels safe and manageable for trauma survivors.

Blending Approaches for Lasting Change

Each of these therapies—CBT, mindfulness, and meditation—offers unique tools that address different facets of trauma. Integrating them with somatic trauma therapy creates a more comprehensive, individualized healing plan that addresses the body, mind, and emotions simultaneously.

When used together, these therapies help individuals:

- **Identify and regulate triggers**: Cognitive awareness combined with somatic grounding makes it easier to identify and manage emotional triggers without becoming overwhelmed.
- **Build emotional resilience**: Mindfulness and meditation practices support long-term emotional regulation by training the mind and body to stay present, grounded, and calm during distress.
- **Process stored trauma**: Somatic techniques allow for the safe release of trauma stored in the body, while CBT provides tools for reframing negative thoughts and building healthier mental habits.

By integrating these therapies, trauma survivors gain a diverse toolkit that addresses both immediate symptoms and underlying trauma patterns, promoting long-lasting recovery and emotional freedom.

Key Takeaway

The integration of somatic trauma therapy with cognitive-behavioral therapy, mindfulness, and meditation offers a holistic and comprehensive approach to trauma healing. By engaging both the mind and body, survivors can regulate their emotions, release stored trauma, and ultimately build a life of resilience and well-being.

VI

Challenges of Somatic Therapy

68

19

Challenges and Solutions in Somatic Therapy

While somatic therapy can be a powerful tool for healing trauma, the process may not always be straightforward. If you're starting or are already working on this approach, it's important to understand the common challenges you may face—and, more importantly, how to overcome them. This chapter will guide you through typical hurdles and offer practical solutions to help you continue your healing journey.

1. Feeling Uncomfortable in Your Body

The Challenge:

For many people, the very act of tuning into their body can be uncomfortable or overwhelming. Trauma often causes us to disconnect from physical sensations as a way to protect ourselves from emotional pain. When starting somatic exercises, this reconnection may bring up sensations or emotions you've been avoiding for years.

Solution:

Take it slow. Start with small practices like mindful breathing or gentle stretches. You don't need to jump into intense body awareness right away. Respect your body's pace and stop when it feels overwhelming. Gradually, you will expand your capacity to stay present with these sensations without feeling too overwhelmed.

2. Overwhelming Emotions

The Challenge:

Somatic therapy taps into stored emotions, which can sometimes lead to an emotional release that feels too intense. You may experience waves of sadness, anger, or even panic during or after a session.

Solution:

It's okay to feel these emotions; they are part of your healing process. If things become too intense, try grounding techniques such as focusing on your breath, touching a solid object, or naming things in your environment. You can also break the process into shorter, manageable sessions to avoid emotional overload.

3. Doubting the Process

The Challenge:

At first, somatic therapy may seem abstract, and you might question whether it's truly helping. Since the effects can take time to manifest, it's easy to feel doubtful or frustrated, especially if you're looking for quick fixes.

Solution:

Be patient with yourself. Healing is not linear, and progress may be slow. Keep track of small wins—whether it's feeling calmer, sleeping better, or noticing a lighter mood. These small victories indicate that change is happening, even if it's not immediately dramatic. Trust the process.

4. Struggling to Stay Consistent

The Challenge:

Life can get busy, and somatic practices can be easy to skip when things feel chaotic or when the exercises seem difficult. Inconsistent practice can slow down the healing process and lead to frustration.

Solution:

Set aside a few minutes each day—5 to 10 minutes is enough—to engage in somatic work. Treat it like brushing your teeth or drinking water; make it a non-negotiable part of your daily routine. If you miss a day, don't be too hard on yourself—just pick it up the next day.

5. Feeling Isolated or Alone in the Journey

The Challenge:

Healing through somatic therapy can feel like a deeply personal, and sometimes lonely, process. If you're not working with a therapist, it may feel like you're carrying this burden on your own.

Solution:

You don't have to go through this journey alone. Consider joining online communities or local support groups where others are working on healing trauma through somatic or other therapeutic practices. Even just reading others' experiences can offer a sense of connection and support. Alternatively, share your experiences with a trusted friend or journal about your journey to process your feelings.

6. *Physical Discomfort or Pain*

The Challenge:

During somatic therapy exercises, you may encounter physical discomfort, such as stiffness, soreness, or even pain in certain areas of your body. This is particularly true if trauma has been stored in your body for a long time.

Solution:

Listen to your body. It's crucial to differentiate between productive discomfort and pain that signals something is wrong. If you feel pain, stop immediately. Modify your exercises to be gentler or focus on another area of your body until you feel ready to revisit that spot. Somatic therapy is about creating safety in your body, not pushing through pain.

7. *Getting Triggered*

The Challenge:

Sometimes, working with trauma stored in the body can trigger old memories or sensations. You might find yourself re-experiencing emotions or physical reactions that seem out of proportion to the present situation.

Solution:

Prepare yourself by learning calming and grounding techniques before diving into more intense somatic work. When triggers arise, remind yourself that you are in the present and safe. After a triggering experience, take some time to recover—this could mean resting, journaling, or talking to someone you trust.

8. *Lack of Immediate Feedback*

The Challenge:

Unlike other therapeutic methods where results might be visible or measurable, somatic therapy often works subtly. The lack of immediate feedback may leave you wondering whether the exercises are "working."

Solution:

Trust that your body knows how to heal. Somatic work often builds up over time. You might not notice progress right away, but small shifts are happening. Be patient, keep a journal of your feelings and physical sensations, and you'll start to notice improvements, even if they seem gradual.

20

Conclusion

Healing from trauma is a journey, one that requires patience, resilience, and self-compassion. By integrating somatic therapy with other therapeutic practices like cognitive-behavioral therapy, mindfulness, and meditation, individuals can address trauma on all levels—emotional, physical, and mental. The power to overcome trauma lies in recognizing that healing is a layered process, with each step building towards a more resilient, peaceful self. As you continue, embrace the courage to confront the past, release stored pain, and move towards a life of freedom, growth, and emotional liberation.

In this journey, remember:

- Healing is not linear but filled with learning moments.
- Your body and mind have the incredible capacity to heal and recover.
- Self-compassion is key in forgiving yourself for what you couldn't control and embracing your full vulnerability as a source of strength.

Let this newfound awareness and commitment to your healing empower you to create a life free from the burdens of past trauma. Keep moving forward, celebrating small victories, and nurturing the incredible progress you've made.

If you found the insights and exercises in this book helpful, your positive review can make a difference. Not only does it support the ongoing creation of helpful resources, but it also encourages others who are embarking on their healing journey. A few words can uplift someone else who may need this book just as much as you did.

Thank you for taking this important step toward healing. Your resilience, courage, and dedication are inspiring, and I'm honored to have been a part of your journey. Wishing you strength and peace as you continue to move forward.

21

Appendices

Appendix A: Glossary of Somatic Therapy Terms

- **Somatic Experiencing (SE)**: A body-focused therapy designed to release trauma through sensations and movement.
- **Grounding**: Techniques used to reconnect individuals to the present moment and their physical body.
- **Emotional Regulation**: Methods that manage and stabilize intense emotions triggered by trauma.
- **Vagus Nerve**: A vital nerve regulating the parasympathetic nervous system, essential in trauma recovery.
- **Body Scan**: A mindfulness practice involving mentally scanning the body to identify and release areas of tension.

Appendix B: Daily Trauma Recovery Plan

Goal: To incorporate somatic practices into daily routines for trauma recovery and emotional well-being.

- **Morning Routine**:
- **Grounding Practice**: Start the day by reconnecting with your body through feet-to-floor grounding or other grounding exercises.
- **Breathwork**: Practice Box Breathing (inhale for 4 counts, hold for 4, exhale for 4, hold for 4) to regulate the nervous system.
- **Gratitude Journal**: Write down three things you're grateful for each morning to foster positivity.
- **Mid-Day Practice**:
- **Quick Somatic Exercise**: Engage in a short body scan or somatic movement exercise like yoga or stretching.
- **Emotional Regulation Technique**: Use the 4-7-8 breathing technique when feeling overwhelmed. This helps center the mind and body.
- **Evening Routine**:
- **Progressive Muscle Relaxation**: Release tension in each muscle group, starting from the feet and working your way up to your head.

- **Safe Space Visualization**: Imagine a peaceful, comforting place where you feel safe, allowing your body to relax before sleep.

Appendix C: Resources and Further Reading

Books:

- *The Body Keeps the Score* by Bessel van der Kolk
- *Waking the Tiger* by Peter Levine

Websites:

- Somatic Experiencing International
- The Trauma Research Foundation

Articles:

- "Understanding the Mind-Body Connection in Trauma" by The National Institute for the Clinical Application of Behavioral Medicine.

Appendix D: Therapist Directory

Finding a Somatic Therapist:

- **International Society for Traumatic Stress Studies (ISTSS)**: A global directory for certified trauma therapists, searchable by region.
- **Somatic Experiencing Practitioners Directory**: Find professionals trained in Somatic Experiencing (SE) therapy.
- **Psychology Today Therapy Directory**: Offers filters to locate trauma-focused therapists, including somatic approaches.

Appendix E: Somatic Therapy Practice Log

Week 1-2: Grounding and Safety

- **Daily Practice**: Record your experiences using grounding techniques such as Feet-to-Floor or Safe Space Visualization.
- **Example Entry**: "After practicing Feet-to-Floor grounding for 10 minutes today, I felt more centered and the tension in my shoulders reduced significantly."

Week 3-4: Releasing Stored Tension

- **Daily Practice**: Focus on releasing physical and emotional tension using Progressive Muscle Relaxation and Shaking Exercises.
- **Example Entry**: "I practiced Progressive Muscle Relaxation before bed, and I noticed that my muscles felt less tight, allowing me to fall asleep faster."